A PEPPER-POD

One autumn day when Bashō and one of his ten disciples, Kikaku, were going through a rice-field, Kikaku composed a haiku on a red dragonfly that caught his fancy. And he showed the following haiku to Bashō:

> Take a pair of wings
> From a dragonfly, you would
> Make a pepper-pod.

"No," said Bashō, "that is not a haiku. You kill the dragon-fly. If you want to compose a haiku and give life to it, you must say:

> Add a pair of wings
> To a pepper-pod, you would
> Make a dragonfly."

— From HAIWA

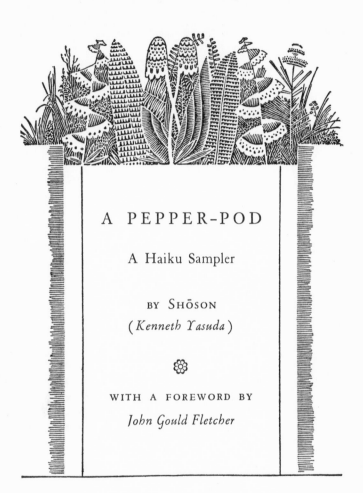

A PEPPER-POD

A Haiku Sampler

BY SHŌSON
(*Kenneth Yasuda*)

❁

WITH A FOREWORD BY
John Gould Fletcher

CHARLES E. TUTTLE COMPANY
Rutland, Vermont & Tokyo, Japan

Representatives

Continental Europe: BOXERBOOKS, INC., *Zurich*

British Isles: PRENTICE-HALL INTERNATIONAL, INC., *London*

Australasia: PAUL FLESCH & CO., PTY. LTD.
c/o Bookwise Australia
104 Sussex Street, Sydney

Canada: HURTIG PUBLISHERS, *Edmonton*

*Published by the Charles E. Tuttle Company, Inc.
of Rutland, Vermont & Tokyo, Japan
with editorial offices at
Suido 1-chome, 2-6, Bunkyo-ku, Tokyo, Japan*

Copyright in Japan, 1976, by Charles E. Tuttle Co., Inc.

International Standard Book No. 0-8048-1114-8

*First edition, 1947 by Alfred A. Knopf, Inc., New York
First Tuttle edition, 1976*

0292-000369-4615
PRINTED IN JAPAN

To Basho and Buson

the author dedicates the present volume in a hope that a bridge may be built between East and West

FOREWORD

A POEM *is always, in whatever language it is written, a pattern of words designed to suggest something to the mind of a reader; and what a poem does suggest — unless it happens to be pure nonsense — is an object existing in time and space. This object may be taken from something existing inside the poet, of which only the poet is fully aware; or it may be taken from something outside, which has appeared to the poet as being an objective parallel to his own inner feelings. Most poems — if not all poems — have in them both kinds of experience: they largely represent, if lyrical in intention, the inner experience of the poet himself, which through a power of magic imagination, amounting to identification, is linked to some external object or occasion, and which acts as a key to unlock that inner experience and to create the pleasures of which the poem is made.*

This is as true of the form of poetry that the Japanese poets call haiku *as it is of any other. The only difference between the Japanese* haiku *poet, and the Western — English or American — poets is this: the Japanese is content to suggest an object, and leaves the resulting emotion for the reader to complete in his own mind. The Western poet states the emotion, along with the object or objects that provoked it; and frequently in stating his emotion, he overdoes* it. This may be the reason why poetry is unpopular among the English or the Americans; and why haiku-making is still popular among the Japanese.

Reading through Mr. Yasuda's skillful translations — and I have never seen any translations of haiku poems which seemed to me to contain so much of the tonal quality of the Japanese — I am again struck, as I was years ago, with the extraordinary power these poems have to set up echoes in the reader's mind, by the use of what Mr. Yasuda wittily calls "versegrams." Only the barest indication, in seventeen syllables, is allowed in the haiku; as for the reason, I must leave the reader to Mr. Yasuda's "Introduction," a magnificent and completely convincing explanation of the subject. These brief "versegrams" — made up of detail which sometimes appears trivial — have a terrific psychological impact, as Mr. Yasuda points out. One is reminded by them of the fact, that had Keats been a Japanese poet, instead of writing an "Ode to a Nightingale" in eight long stanzas, all he need have written were the two best lines: —

> Charmed magic casements, opening on the foam
> Of perilous seas, in faery lands forlorn.

I have already referred to the seeming triviality of the detail in many of these haiku poems. This is bound to be the besetting fault of any art so widely known, popular, and universally practised as the haiku is among the Japanese; while the corresponding virture of the haiku art is that in its best examples no word is wasted (as it is in so many Western poems) and the object described as well as the feel-

ing expressed are absolutely one (as in so many of Bashō's poems). Western poems, on the contrary, do not suffer from triviality of detail; in fact, the detail — thanks to the wider range of the Western form — frequently overwhelms and swamps the subject.

Mr. Yasuda, who writes under the pen-name of Shōson, a name made up from the last syllables of the names of Bashō and Buson, the two most celebrated haiku *poets, seems to me the only translator of the many whom I have read in German, French, or English, who understands fully the spirit as well as the letter of the* haiku *form. Mr. Yasuda is an educated and cultivated Japanese-American, which is his advantage over the others who have previously attempted to translate* haiku *poems into English; just as it is his personal misfortune, at the present moment, to be a Japanese-American, since we have been, so recently, at war with Japan. However, I happen to think that this misfortune — which Mr. Yasuda shares with thousands of others — will, in the long run, be overweighed by the advantages. We, though we have succeeded in conquering the Japanese people, can never destroy them completely, and will in fact have to learn from them, as they can learn from us, now that this war is finished. What we can learn — since we are far from perfect — is important; and a great deal of it is stated and suggested in Mr. Yasuda's translations and experimental adaptations, as well as in his introductory essay. It is something that may help to lead poetry back to first principles, which surely should come first; and should lead some of the more intelligent moderns to cast* off the burden of too-conscious intellectualism that they carry. For the merit of these haiku poems is not only that they suggest much by saying little; they also, if understood in connection with the Zen doctrine they illuminate, make of poetry an act of life.

JOHN GOULD FLETCHER

Little Rock
January 18, 1946

ACKNOWLEDGMENT

Acknowledgment is due to Kyoshi Takahama, the *haiku*-poet, the editor of the book entitled *Shin Saijiki*. I have selected *haiku* from it for the present volume. I wish to express my appreciation of the valuable help rendered me by Professor A. Miyamori. His works have been of great service. I owe my thanks to Dr. D. Griffith, Dr. L. Zilman, and Professor George Savage of the University of Washington for their useful and frank criticism. Also my heartfelt thanks are due to John Gould Fletcher, who read the entire manuscript and kindly wrote a foreword to this volume. Finally, I wish to express my appreciation for the sustained interest and encouragement shown by Sada Murayama, without whose inspiration this book could not have seen the light.

S. K. Y.

CONTENTS

INTRODUCTION

EACH time I look at an old picture painted on rich silk
by Chinese painters of the T'an Dynasty, and especially one
of the monochrome paintings in Chinese ink by such a mas-
ter as Wang Wei or some later masters of the Sung period, it
moves me strongly. The effect of the picture, in black and
white and with subtle gradation from white to black, is of
mysticism and extreme delicacy. Unlike an oil painting, it
fills the space without filling it, as when a sampan rises out
of a silver mist of the Yangtse river, the faint outlines of dis-
tant mountains appear far beyond, and a pagoda's darker
lines float between and above the misty veil over the rich
valley.

A picture, whether a portrait or a scene as described
above, can be enjoyed just by looking at it. Painting is easy
to appreciate, even for those who are illiterate. No special
knowledge is required: at a glance one can feel all that is
there. This is called "intuition." Thus any work of colors
is to be esteemed, praised, valued through this act of imme-
diate perception of beauty without conscious effort or rea-
soning.

The same holds true of poetry and especially of *haiku,* a
one-breath poem in three lines, a single flower of beauty
whose petals are seventeen syllables, all told. Enjoyment
that we receive from this telegraphic poem comes intui-

tively rather than through logical reasoning. For instance, in the *haiku:*

> Autumn evening now:
> A crow alone is perching
> On the leafless bough.[1]

We feel intrinsically that the air is clear in the above poem; the skies hang gently above the horizon like a cobalt mirror. There, against its tranquil background of autumn blue turning almost into deep purple, we can see the tall tree standing, distinct and still, above the gathering gloom of the autumn twilight, and a black crow perching alone on one of the withered branches. A loneliness is there, and a mystic power that holds us close with an acute feeling akin to a melancholy sadness.

(1) Autumn evening, (2) a crow, (3) and the leafless bough — these three have the same feeling, and we are moved by and impressed with this common emotion existing among them; and through them, alone and only, can we feel that emotion by a sense of intuition.

Here we want no adjective to blur our impression — the picture speaks for itself. We seek no metaphor or simile to make the picture impressive, but let the objects do their part. If the picture is beautiful, so that he who looks must admire, how superfluous and intrusive it would sound if the author were to exclaim, "Oh, how beautiful it is — etc." If it is sad, we do not want him to tell us so, but demand that he make it sad: our own appreciation will supply the necessary adjectives.

[1] See page 8.

Indeed, simple treatment of this kind, whether of a picture or of a poem, is always the most difficult of all. It demands a true and mature artist like the above poet, Bashō himself.

> Underneath the eaves
> Large hydrangeas' clustered disks
> Overbrim the leaves.[2]

Here we see the hydrangea growing with the large disks of clustered flowers by the house. "Overbrim the leaves" the poet writes, to say figuratively how the flowers bloom among and above the deep green enameled leaves. It has bright light; it gives the impression of a rich oil painting drawn with the dynamic strokes of a masterful hand.

> Scattered, the peony:
> One beside another pile,
> Petals two or three.[3]

This is an equally colorful picture. The beauty of the splendid peony is expressed in itself. The richness of the flower has a magic touch to keep our attention; yet here, viewing its large petals piled one beside another, we feel a new charm characteristic of the peony; moreover, the opening rhythm heightens its effect. With a dynamic cadence, how appropriate it is to begin by saying, "Scattered . . ."! By the verb "pile" its movement is held with a sense of weight exquisitely enough to give the living impression of the petals that *pile* one *beside* the other, rather than that *lie* one *above* the other. This impression is further vivified by

[2] See page 118.   [3] See page 49.

the definite image of the number of the petals ("two or three" in the concluding line), giving the concrete impression to the reader.

> Crimson dragonfly,
> As it lights, sways together
> With a blade of rye.[4]

If we make this poem a painting, such a simple and delightful picture on rich silk as we find in some old Oriental scrolls, the delicacy of this mode of expression with words is beyond the touch of even the masterful hand and brush, especially that instant when the dragonfly comes to rest and, by its own weight, sways in unison with the slender blade of rye. Also, the feeling that comes from the harmonious motion of the object cannot be made visual or tangible to our senses, nor is it possible to suggest it adequately and delicately as this poem expressed it in a poetic rhythm in a mode particular to itself.

> In the twilight gloom
> Of the redwood and the pine
> Fair wisterias bloom.[5]

Here is a twilight touch of scenic beauty; the lovely wisterias hang their clusters against the background of the semi-darkness of the redwood and the pine, whereby the rich purple of the flowers gains its softness and its visual contrast. It reminds us of the rich coloring of some exotic painting, especially of the Southern School of Wang Wei in the Sung period.

[4] See page 111. [5] See page 90.

Thus *haiku* has something in common with painting. "Comparing it with painting," says Professor A. Miyamori, "the *haiku* is like a sketch or the outline of a sketch — the *haiku* is the title of a picture, nay, a suggestion for one." How true his statement is, but a moment's consideration of the first poem by Bashō shows that the picture painted, however brief in itself, is more than a sketch or the title of a picture.

Let us suppose, for instance, we receive a radiogram or telegram saying: "ILL, COME HOME." These three words contain more meaning than the words themselves convey or than any picture that one may draw! This telegraphic expression, which we use in everyday business life for all purposes other than poetic, is nevertheless one of the prominent characteristics of *haiku* because pregnancy and suggestiveness, brevity and ellipsis, are the soul and life of a *haiku*. So a *haiku* may be called a "versegram."

Now we are ready to compare this versegram more critically with painting by analyzing the parts. Let us take the following example:

> White swans, one or two,
> Draw near, pushing the water
> For the food I threw.[6]

Suppose that a painter sees the above poem. He will draw one or two swans facing the food, and a few curved lines in front of the birds denoting the waves or ripples in such a way to give the impression of swans approaching.

[6] See page 119.

Painting thus makes us visualize the moment of action or movement by *presenting* a certain desirable form and appropriate position of the object in space; on the other hand, a versegram gives that spatial form by *stating* the movement of the object with such a phrase as "pushing the water." Consequently it may be said that painting is always spatial, and *haiku* temporal. That is the fundamental difference between them as far as their mode of expression is concerned; yet, analyzing *haiku* further, one may soon discover that it is more an art of "line and form" than painting, because in it we find a more distinct realization of space, direction, dimension, atmosphere, and perspective in scene or landscape.

This world of *haiku* consists of seventeen syllables. It is as restricted in scope as a few square inches of silk or paper. *Haiku,* however, is three-dimensional.

Now you may ask: how can one paint a picture in words with only seventeen syllables? How can one thus describe and denote the space, time, distance, dimension, perspective, etc., that we find in every painting? These and many other similar questions may be asked.

To answer these questions, I may suggest that the verb gives us the elements of perspective; and also that words like spring, summer, noon, evening, vesper, aurora, and many others indicate time; words such as far and near suggest distance; right, left, beginning, middle, end, etc., denote the direction and position of the object. In addition, poetry may employ many other imaginable methods to give the perspective elements we find in painting.

INTRODUCTION

But it may seem that in the *haiku* world of seventeen syllables there would be insufficient room for crowding together the words needed to denote — or at least hint at — the elements in question.

It may also seem impossible to add the third dimension to the *haiku* world we hope to create with beautiful words. Yet as long as *haiku* is the true picture of what we see in nature, the artist must convey the elements of perspective, no matter how small and microscopic the world of *haiku* may be. So the question, "How shall I accomplish this end to make *haiku* pure art?" would be difficult to answer. However, a moment of reflection on the art of painting gives us a hint through which we may get a clear concept of the *haiku* world, because there can be no art of any sort without composition, whether done consciously or unconsciously.

The artist reduces all things in nature to a two-dimensional world on silk or paper, but he places the objects in their positions exactly as they are: he uses the true phenomena of nature and sees the trees nearby taller than the trees far away, as in Kou Hsi's concept of "three dimensions" in painting. Kou Hsi said precisely: "Clear distinct figures should not be short; fine and definite ones not too tall; mild and dreamy ones not too large. These are the laws of three dimensions." So let us suppose Hokusai, the famous painter, draws a picture of Buson's poem:

> O, the rains of spring!
> An umbrella and raincoat
> Pass by, conversing.[7]

[7] See page 49.

INTRODUCTION

No doubt with a few subtle strokes he will draw a simple picture in which we shall see the two persons, one with an umbrella and the other with a raincoat, and also a few dozen lines slanting down from above, indicating the rain. The rain is above the umbrella and raincoat. In the painting these objects must be kept as they are; otherwise the picture will lose its perspective. This is also true in *haiku,* and they must be kept in *this* order. Observe carefully:

> O, the rains of spring!
> An umbrella and raincoat
> Pass by, conversing.

We see the rain *above* the umbrella and raincoat! Thus, composition in *haiku* has the same importance as design in painting. What I mean by "composition" here is that act of organizing thoughts within the limited space of only seventeen syllables in order to create one lovely picture.

The poem already quoted may be used to further illustrate this:

> White swans, one or two,
> Draw near, pushing the water
> For the food I threw.

Here a poet placed the swans at the far end as the painter would draw them; the ripples are expressed figuratively by a phrase, "pushing the water," and the position of the birds is indicated by the verb draw and the adverb near. This is further pointed out and the relations are made clear and distinct, by placing the food in the third line as it would be in a painting.

Haiku is the true scene reduced to a two-dimensional world in word-print on paper, but the natural order and the position of the objects are kept unaltered by the word order. As soon as the time element is introduced by the movement of our eyes along the lines and the time we require to read the words, the *haiku* world becomes a three-dimensional world; therefore, as we read *haiku*, every object reduced to print begins to rise, and we see clearly the trees in their own position and heights. The mountains, the lakes, and all that may be found in the *haiku* world take their respective place in natural order. Thus, things in *haiku* become alive before the reader.

According to this concept of three dimensions, I classify *haiku* into three groups: vertical, horizontal, and diagonal, or a blend of both. The *haiku* of Buson cited above belongs to the vertical class and the swan poem to the horizontal. Another example of the second class may be given here:

> On the bench I wait
> For the second gust to come
> Through the garden gate.[8]

We see the *bench* at the one end and the *gate* at the other. Between there is nothing, but the cool summer gust can pass freely at evening.

> In moonlight, half-hid
> With the silhouettes of leaves
> Twits the katydid.[9]

This poem at first seems vertical, since we might see the moon above everything else; but the moon is not at its

[8] See page 125.   [9] See page 112.

zenith because it is then impossible to have vivid silhouettes. Therefore we must consider that the moon, in this case, is at the far end. For this reason, this *haiku* world is horizontal. The position of the moon, in this horizontal *haiku* world, indicates the time distinctly: it is the rising moon. It can be assumed, however, that the moon's position is high enough to give the clearest aspect of the *haiku* world. Consequently we may classify this poem in the third group.

Observing the perspective in this poem, we notice that the poet puts the leaves as close to the insect as possible, indicating that some of the leaves are in front of and some behind the katydid. This is further indicated by the word half-hid, and also by the plural silhouettes. Suppose we change the natural order of the things, i.e., the word order, in the following manner:

> From the leaves, half-hid
> In the silhouettes of moon,
> Twits the katydid.

Then we have: (1) leaves, (2) silhouettes — moon, (3) katydid in this jumbled order, which is not natural; and when we add the third dimension to this picture by reading the poem, the horizontal and vertical *haiku* world cannot be created immediately, except by the act of synthesis. This mental process, however, decreases the æsthetic pleasure proportionally to the effort required to place the objects in their natural position and order. In order to make *haiku* a pure art, this order must be kept, and the poet must maintain the natural position of the objects in a poem. This was indicated by Herbert Spencer in his essay entitled "The Philosophy of Style." He said: "A reader or listener has at each moment but a limited amount of mental power available. To recognize and interpret the syllables represented to him, requires part of this power; to arrange and combine the images suggested by them requires a further part; and only that part which remains can be used for framing the thought expressed. Hence, the more time and attention it takes to receive and understand each sentence, the less time and attention can be given to the contained idea; and the less vividly will that idea be conceived." Thus it becomes clear that by physical necessity the order of the words is important and it is the only means by which the immediate perception of beauty in a poem can be made possible. This order is what I call "*haiku* movement." It is one of the important elements of *haiku* besides seventeen syllables and reference to the season. *Haiku* is three-dimensional, and everything in this telegraphic poem is alive.

At this point the reader may ask: why must *haiku* be written in seventeen syllables in three lines? I have often heard this question, and no one has yet given a satisfactory answer to it. However, let me briefly state here what I have learned.

I shall attempt to answer the above question by asking you a very simple question. "Did you ever see a scene or a thing that affected you in such a way that you were one with it?" I know when one happens to see a beautiful sunset or lovely flowers, for instance, he will be so delighted that he merely stands still. This state of mind is what I call "ah-ness," which will constitute an æsthetic experience, a basis for a telegraphic poem.

It is always a single event. The duration of this single event, of "ah-ness," is a breath's length by physical necessity, so far as we are concerned. In this state of "ah-ness" Schopenhauer said, "He who contemplates the beautiful forgets even his individuality, his will, and only continues to exist as the pure subject, the clear mirror of the object." *Haiku* poets try to produce this state of "ah-ness" in the mind of readers by presenting only the essentials reflected on that mirror. So in order to produce the exact effects upon the reader, the length of the line for *haiku* thought in *haiku* expression must have the same length as the duration of the single event of "ah-ness," which is a breath's length. Consequently, the length of a verse is made up of those groups of words which we can utter during one breath. The length, that is, is necessitated by *haiku* nature and by the physical impossibility of pronouncing an unlimited number of syllables in a given period.

To a reader, that moment of inspiration or state of "ah-ness" comes only after such groups of words are read, and it can be completed only at the end of the poem. During a breath's period he reads; tensions are harmoniously maintained in rhythmic continuity to elevate his soul, and as he pauses at the end of the verse, the sense of inner strains dies out, giving a feeling of perfect finality no less exquisite and beautiful than the state of "ah-ness" that the poet first conceived. In this way *haiku* re-creates the true image of beauty in the mind of the reader. Thus the length of a line may be expressed by the number of the syllables that can be uttered in a breath during the state of "ah-ness."

Now let us read in one breath lines from famous poets:

Under yonder beech-tree single on the greensward,
Couched with her arms behind her golden hair . . .
George Meredith

Come and show me another city with lifted head singing
So proud to be alive and coarse and strong and cunning.
Carl Sandburg

Once when the snow of the year was beginning to fall,
We stopped by a mountain pasture to say, "whose colt?"
Robert Frost

These are a little too long to be read at a breath. Let us try the following line or lines:

More precious was the light in your eyes than the roses in
the world
Edna St. Vincent Millay

It was many and many a year ago
In the kingdom of the sea.
Edgar Allan Poe

I must down to the seas again, to the lonely sea and the sky
John Masefield

We shall find that the longest lines in English to be read at one breath contain between sixteen and eighteen syllables. This is true not only in English, but also in the other languages. For instance, the songs written in the antique tongue employed by Homer in the *Iliad* and *Odyssey* and by Virgil in the *Æneid* are both in dactylic hexameter. And in *Evangeline,* imitated in a classic meter by Longfellow, the meter consists of five dactyls and a final trochee, varying the number of syllables from sixteen to eighteen. So we can say that the number of syllables that can be said in a breath makes the natural length of *haiku*. This is why *haiku* is written in seventeen syllables.

It is not necessary, however, to write *haiku* only in seventeen syllables. It may be permissible to use fifteen or eighteen syllables, both of which can be pronounced in a breath, but we must remember that *haiku* is subjected to rhythm.

The rhythm in *haiku* demands that the poet divide a line of seventeen syllables into three parts to justify his sense of balance. The first line of five syllables and the third line of the same number give the quality of symmetry. The proportion between the first line and the second creates a most pleasing relationship between them, what we call "rhythmic-half," that is one half of the first part goes into the second part approximately three times; and this proportion is almost like that of the golden section. Our reference to such proportion in *haiku* is an expression of the desire for balance that will obtain a quality of pleasantness. "The cause of this is not the demand merely for an equality of ratios," said Professor Winter, "but a demand merely for greater variety." [10] The effort to secure variety that pleases us leads us to consider rhythmic elements in the temporal pattern of the *haiku* form.

We find that the form for *haiku* thought follows a mathematical pattern: a line of from sixteen to eighteen syllables

[10] *Analytical Psychology,* by Winter.

divided into three parts or lines in such a way that the first is the same length as the third, and one half of the first goes into the second three times, i.e., the three parts are in an approximate relation of 5, 7, and 5 syllables. This is the reason why the *haiku* is a breath-poem of three lines, a single flower of beauty whose petals are seventeen syllables.

This brings us to consider *haiku* rhythm. Let us take the following poem to analyze the rhythm:

> Brushing the leaves, fell
> A camellia into the soft
> Darkness of the well.[11]

In this poem it will be noted how harmoniously the feeling in rhythm is expressed through the dual nature of language, its union of *sound elements* and *thought elements*, true to the poet's feeling about the movement or motion of the object, in this case a camellia. I shall call the rhythm of the former "latitudinal rhythm," and the rhythm of the latter, "longitudinal rhythm." Accordingly, the longitudinal rhythm signifies the rhythm of thought as the meaning of idea externalized in temporal order by means of words used. It is therefore measured or counted by the number of syllables in accordance with the flow of thought within a line, or from one line to the other. Consequently, its characteristic rhythm in each line is called *"haiku tune."* The latitudinal rhythm means the rhythm of feeling as the pulsation of thought; and it is expressed by means of the tone quality of sound or accent in the word that vivifies the longitudinal rhythm.

[11] See page 105.

The flow of thought in the above poem may be divided as follows:

> Brushing the leaves
> fell
> a camellia
> into the soft darkness
> of the well

The participial phrase "brushing the leaves" may be further divided into two parts, "brushing" and "the leaves," according to the flow of thought. So the *haiku* tune in the first line may be shown thus by counting syllables: 2:2:1:

> Brushing the leaves, fell.
> ————————————————
> 2   2   1

Accordingly, the second line in this manner: 4:2:2:

> A camellia into the soft,
> ————————————————
> 4   2   2

and the last line thus: 2:1:2:

> Darkness of the well.
> ————————————————
> 2   1   2

This reveals the following facts: as the unit of the longitudinal rhythm must be the same as the unit of our thought-flow, it is represented by a word of one syllable, for the unit of our thought is a word of one syllable, since the unit of a word is a syllable of one. But as in music two units are required to form a measure, so rhythm demands for its formation at least two, no less than the unit of "rhythmic-half." Consequently, in the formation of a thought-rhythm, our thought tends to flow in this basic measure of "rhythmic-half," with its unit of one syllable, and the combination of both or their multiple is the basic measure in *haiku*. Therefore, *haiku* tune in the first line and in the third line has the following possibilities in general: (a) ·1:2:2, (b) 2:1:2, and (c) 2:2:1. And in the second line the following syllabic combination in general is possible: (a) 1:2:2:2, (b) 2:1:2:2, (c) 2:2:1:2, and (d) 2:2:2:1. These *haiku* tunes have their own characteristics, but they vary in accordance with the mood and feeling in each case.

Now we shall come back to the poem:

> Brushing the leaves, fell
> A camellia into the soft
> Darkness of the well

and examine the effect of *haiku* tune upon the harmony existing between longitudinal and latitudinal rhythms.

The first line is characterized by the longitudinal rhythm in a *haiku* tune of 2:2:1 as we have already seen:

Brushing the leaves, fell.		
2	2	1

This *haiku* tune progresses evenly in 2:2 and at the very end changes into 1 instead of 2, which gives an irregular effect to the flow of rhythm; and by the meaning of the word fell this irregular movement of feeling in temporal order gains its meaning as a sudden drop, true to the motion of the falling of the camellia-flower.

Viewing *haiku* tune in contrast to as well as in combination with the latitudinal rhythm, will soon show how intricate is the design of *haiku*. This *haiku* tune of 2:2:1 is vivified or intensified by the accents of words in perfect harmony with the movement of the object, the falling of the camellia-flower, which is the principal substance of the *haiku* rhythm in this poem:

Brushing the leaves, fell

Here the trochaic opening of this line is followed by an iambic movement. This creates a rich and smooth trough as an action of "brushing" itself, with the two unaccented syllables between those two crests of ictus in the forward progression of thought as *haiku* tune of 2:2. It is followed in succession by the accented syllable "fell," making the abrupt and sudden ending that gives the true effect of the camellia-flower dropping. Moreover, from the meaning of the word fell the rhythmic flow of the first line is made to ebb into the second line as though "What fell?":

A camellia into the soft.

The first syllable, "A," harmonizing with the one syllable of "fell" (which produces lack of one syllable at the end of the first line) satisfies the rhythmic succession of the basic measure of 2. From the meaning as thought-flow it also makes a multiple of 2 by adding 1 to "A" and 3 in "camellia" for the rhythmic flow of the second line. The three syllables in the word camellia itself give body and weight to subject as the center of interest, and distinctly stamp on our mind the positive impression of the large red image of the flower, as significant as possible in contrast with the background of the "soft darkness" into which it falls. The rest of the line flows in a *haiku* tune of 2:2 in a harmonious unison with the metrical rhythm, colored by the half-accented stress:

—————— into the soft.

This half-accented trochaic flow of "into," followed by the half-accented iambic ebb of "the soft," carries the object into the last line:

Darkness of the well.

Here the forceful trochaic beginning is softened by the preceding half-accented stress of "soft" at the end of the second line. The long trough created by the unaccented syllables between the two crests at the beginning and the end suggest the deep passage of the well filled with the soft darkness into which the camellia fell. In the forward movement of the thought rhythm in *haiku* tune of 2:1:2

Darkness of the well —
2   1   2

it also makes us feel, with its sense of balance and the conclusive character of the *haiku* tune, that the falling camellia-flower comes to rest. Finally, the last word, "well," which rhymes with the word "fell" at the end of the first line, recalls the whole movement by its echoes, giving the vivid impression of finality and of the completeness of the *haiku* cadence in a harmonious cycle.

Here the rhyme plays an important part. It is the most obvious way to emphasize the pulsation of feeling and meaning, for the definite repetition of accented vowel and subsequent sound produces a synchronous vibration when two words rhyme with each other. It not only produces the above effect, but also gives concreteness to *haiku* form as a frame does to a picture. Those words which rhyme are usually, in excellent *haiku,* the key words vital to the *haiku.* For example, the word "fell" in the above *haiku,* which rhymes with the word "well," asks "what fell" and by its lyric echo brings to us once more the whole cadence.

Before we come back to *haiku* rhythm, let us take a few examples and see how the rhymed words are the key words in the poem:

> Hurriedly runs rain
> Toward the sunlit grain-field
> Half-across the plain.[12]

In this poem the key word is the rain that hides half of the plain as it hurries toward the shining green waves of the grain. Here the word "rain" is used as the center of interest, from and around which this lovely action and scene are created. *It points out directly the center of the interest.* The rhyme also acts as the key to the *haiku* movement when the rhyming words are those that express some action or movement as the word "fell" as in the camellia-poem.

Another function of rhyme is to vivify or intensify the center of interest, instead of pointing it out directly to the reader. For example:

[12] See page 116.

In the twilight gloom
Of the redwood and the pine
Fair wisterias bloom.

There is a twilight touch of scenic beauty; the lovely wisterias hang their clusters against the background of semi-darkness of the redwood and the pine. Here the verb "bloom" brings out the rich purple of the clusters of wis-teria-flowers, and as it rhymes with "twilight-gloom," it places the flowers against this rich, soft darkness. Thus the "twilight gloom," serving as the background, vivifies the visual contrast, and the softness of the purple color of the wisteria comes out into the foreground most effectively.

The following poem will illustrate how rhyme intensi-fies the center of interest:

In the lonely night
There the firefly glides one foot,
Putting out its light.[13]

Here the firefly's light holds our attention as the center of interest. This "light" is intensified by the rhyming word, "night," in the first line because its lonely darkness brings out the "light" of the firefly most effectively. This effect of intensification is due to the association of the contrasting ideas in the rhymed words. The association of allied or kin-dred ideas may be used for rhyme as well, for example:

Luminous and cool
Is the way the pebble sinks
Into the blue pool.[14]

[13] See page 30.   [14] See page 105.

The blue pool into which the little pebble sinks gives us a refreshing feeling by itself, and moreover the word "cool" that rhymes with "pool" enlivens that feeling once more and animates our whole being. The idea-rhyme placed with the sound-rhyme, as in this case, is the ideal concept of rhyme in *haiku,* and when this is achieved without any strain, we are charmed and enchanted by its spell.

For these reasons I use rhyme in all of my *haiku.*

Now let us come back to *haiku* rhythm. I shall use the famous *haiku* entitled "At My Hut" [15] by Bashō:

> Is the bell that booms
> Ueno, Asakusa ——
> Beyond cherry brumes? [16]

The *haiku* tune of this first line is 1:2:2. The increasing number of syllables as this *haiku* tune progresses gives us the effect of rising, inspiring, and expanding feeling as true as the sound of the temple-bell tolled at evening. The accent in this line is appropriate, for its regular beat sets the quiet atmosphere; it also suggests the even tolling of the bell. The second line flows in the *haiku* tune of 3:4:

$$\frac{\text{Ueno, Asakusa ——}}{3 \qquad 4}$$

This *haiku* tune is peculiar and exclusively its own because it translates the feeling of the sound of the bell with its expanding rhythm in a *haiku* tune of 3:4. This 3, which is

[15] Titles in this book are the author's; no titles are given the originals.
[16] See page 9.

the combination of 1 and 2, and this 4, the multiple of the basic measure 2, seem to suggest vividly the rich and sonorous echoing of the bell coming through the cherry-mist as the sound expands in the evening air. Furthermore, the latitudinal rhythm, which flows like a liquid without any marked accent or stress,[17] brings out the trailing sound of the temple-bell as subtly as the inspiring deep gong of the huge bell itself coming through the mist of the blooming cherries.

The last line, in contrast to the rhythm of the first line, ends in the falling rhythm of the *haiku* tune of 2:2:1:

Beyond cherry brumes;

2   2   1

and the iambic beginning of the last line, in latitudinal rhythm,

Bĕyónd chérry brŭmes

leads our attention onward and carries us to the farther side by the flow of the flowing rhythm in amphnaceh, where the last word ("brumes") rhymes with the word ("blooms") at the end of the first line. This brings to us once more the voice of the temple-bell as vividly as it comes through the cherry-mist in a lyric echo of its rhyme as the cadence of *haiku*.

The rhythm in *haiku* moves in circles, as can be seen in the above example. The use of accent, the vocal stress on a syllable, in *haiku* is different from that in general metrical

---

[17] The Japanese language has no accent or stress such as we find in English.

verse. Its chief function is not to secure meter, but to enhance the *haiku* movement, true to both the thought and the emotional ebb and flow in the original pulsation. This is used in order to bring out the rhythm inherent in every thought, however simple or subtle, and in every feeling, however evanescent or profound. Therefore, the accent falls where the pulsation demands instead of being placed upon the stressed syllables to secure meter.

The cadenced line in *haiku* cannot be attained by a mere arrangement of accented and unaccented syllables. It must Le organized in the way by which the pulsation of the thought and feeling forces the poet to translate it in an organic whole. The movement of the cadenced line in *haiku* is not like the movement in, let us say, tap-dancing. It is more like that in Nō dancing, the movement of posture that does not follow the regular pattern, but conforms to thought and rhythm peculiar to itself. For this reason, *haiku* rhythm cannot be easily noticed, nor is it as simple as metrical rhythm.

It will be noted that there are two rhythms in *haiku,* latitudinal and longitudinal, together constituting the *haiku* rhythm. The former is emotional in its quality, and is expressed by means of sound in words. The latter is intellectual, and is vivified and colored by the emotional characters of the former, namely by accent, rhyme, dissonance, assonance, and alliteration. So the longitudinal rhythm may appear to us to be pushed into the background by the various methods of emphasis in latitudinal rhythm, and the vibration of the feeling may seem to come into the foreground as the true original feeling aroused by the objects expressed in the world of *haiku*.

Haiku is an embodiment of realism and impressionism — like painting. *Haiku* poets show us, as we have seen, the objects that excite emotions. They do not express feelings aroused by the objects, but let the objects excite us; they exhibit or present, rather than describe, the concrete individual things because only those have power upon our feelings.

Description, however detailed and vivid, does not make us see anything in the true sense of the word, whereas exhibiting the particular emotional power residing in things or scenes gives us the value of "significance" by the imaginative influence of the whole through the *haiku* rhythm. For this reason, moreover, the poet does not *describe* all he *sees,* but *renders* in a few epithets what he *feels,* so that imagination will fill the spaces with all details in which the emotional value of the images resides and which are to be the permanent possession of our memory. Consequently, the images in our memory are nothing but those that come from objects directly: for every object in nature has its natural expression that intrinsically stamps a certain impression on our mind. Indeed, in this expression the *haiku* poet tries to render directly the things before us just as they are, through *haiku* rhythm and in a most appropriate manner, i.e., like painting, without any coloring from his mind. *Haiku,* as I have said, is a "versegram," a one breath poem in three lines, a single flower of beauty whose petals are seventeen syllables, all told. When we see such a poem, how true is it that "the meanest flower can give thoughts that do often lie too deep for tears."

I hope that this shows "what *haiku* is" and that the *haiku* form will prove to be one of the means of writing poems that "should be equal to," and poems that "should not mean . . . But be," as Archibald MacLeish said in his famous "Ars Poetica."

S. K. Y.

Columbia University
February 25, 1946

PART ONE

TRANSLATIONS INTO ENGLISH

BY SHŌSON

ON HAIKU

> It's a flash of thought
> That winds my throat to make me
> Utter one brief note.
>
> Shōson

A PEPPER-POD

TRANSLATIONS INTO ENGLISH

A BUTTERFLY

A falling flower, thought I,
Flew back to the branch, but oh,
'Twas a butterfly.

Ah today the hour
Of my life appears a small
Morning-glory flower.

Rakka eda ni
Kaeruto mireba
Kochō kana
Moritake
  (1472–1549)

Asagao ni
Kyō wa miyuran
Waga yo kana
Moritake

3

MOUNT FUJI

For the Happy New
Year's Day I'd keep Mount Fuji
As a special view.

HARVEST MOON

Only if we can
Add a handle to the moon
It would make a good fan !

LESPEDEZA–FLOWERS

Lespedezas bend
With the flowers and there the stream
Flows at meadow-end.

Ganjitsu no	Tsuki ni e wo	Hana wo omomi
Miru mono ni sen	Sashi taraba yoki	Hagi ni mizu yuku
Fuji no yama	Uchiwa kana	Nozue kana
Sōkan (1458–1546)	*Sōkan*	*Shōha*
		(1521–1600)

4

IN THE AUTUMN

In the autumn we
Hear the insects' songs that shower
Tintinnabulously.

THE CHERRY BLOSSOMS OF MT. YOSHINO

Nothing but "oh, oh !"
All that I can say on cherry-
Blossomed Yoshino.

THE BRIGHT MOON

The moon at midnight
May be a sphere of coolness
Shining full and bright.

Aki wa mushi wo
Kiku ya shigure no
Chinchirori
Teitoku
(1570–1653)

Korewa korewa
To bakari hana no
Yoshino-yama
Teishitsu
(1609–1673)

Suzushisa no
Katamari nare ya
Yoha no tsuki
Teishitsu

THE SUMMER MOOR

Through summer grasses
Nought is seen but pilgrim's staff
As on he passes.

RIVER MISTS

River mists that float
On the wind, look soft and light
From the loading-boat.

THE CRYSTAL SPRING

To my own scooping
Hands the leaves of oak-tree move
In the crystal spring.

Junrei no
Bō bakari yuku
Natsuno kana
Shigeyori

Kaze no noru
Kawagiri karoshi
Takase bune
Sō-in (1604–1682)

Musubu te ni
Kashi no ha ugoku
Shimizu kana
Sō-in

6

UNCONFESSED LOVE

"Summer thinness, dear,"
I replied to him and then
Burst into a tear.

VIEWING CHERRY-FLOWERS

Looking at the fair
Cherries, with a servant, I
Plod on here and there.

KITES

In the evening sky
Clouds seem melancholy, where
Kites are flying high.

Natsu yase to	Ichi boku to	Yūgure no
Kotaete ato wa	Bokuboku ariku	Mono uki kumo ya
Namida kana	Hanami kana	Iganobori
Kigin (1623-1705)	*Kigin*	*Saimaru*

THE ANCIENT POND

Ancient pond unstirred
Into which a frog has plunged,
A splash was heard.

A CROW ON A BARE BRANCH

Autumn evening now:
A crow alone is perching
On a leafless bough.

WISTERIA FLOWER

Weary, at the hour
I seek a resting place, I
Find wisteria-flower.

Furuike ya	Kare-eda ni	Kutabirete
Kawazu tobikomu	Karasu no tomari keri	Yadokaru koro ya
Mizu no oto	Aki no kure	Fuji no hana
Bashō (1644–1694)	*Bashō*	*Bashō*

8

AT MY HUT

Is the bell that booms
Ueno, Asakusa —
Beyond cherry-brumes?

THE GALAXY

Wild the rolling sea !
Over which to Sado Isle
Lies the Galaxy.

THE FIRST SNOW

Oh, the first soft snow !
Enough to bend the lovely
Leaves of jonquil low.

Hana no kumo	Ara-umi ya	Hatsu yuki ya
Kane wa Ueno ka	Sado ni yokoto	Suisen no ha no
Asakusa ka	Ama no kawa	Tawamu made
Bashō	*Bashō*	*Bashō*

9

CICADA'S SHRILL

How silent and still !
Into the heart of rocks sinks
The cicada's shrill.

AUTUMN WINDS

If one speaks, he finds
How chilly the lips would be
In the autumn winds.

THE RIVER MOGAMI

Gathering rains of May,
The River Mogami rushes
Swiftly on her way.

Shizukasa ya	Mono ieba	Samidare wo
Iwa ni shimi-iru	Kuchibiru samushi	Atsumete hayashi
Semi no koe	Aki no kaze	Mogami gawa
Bashō (1644–1694)	*Bashō*	*Bashō*

ON THE MOUNTAIN TRAIL

From plum-scented veil
Of haze suddenly rose the sun
On the mountain trail.

AT ISE SHRINE

Although from what fair
Flowers it came I can not guess,
Fragrance fills the air !

THE CICADA

In the cicada's cry
There's no sign that can foretell
How soon it must die.

Umega ka ni	Nan no ki no	Yagate shinu
Notto hi no deru	Hanatowa arazu	Keshiki wa miezu
Yamaji kana	Nioi kana	Semi no koe
Bashō	*Bashō*	*Bashō*

AUTUMN CHESTNUT

Though the autumn wind
Blows, the chestnut burrs are green
On the twig I find.

HARVEST MOON

Oh, moon, fair and bright,
Sea-waves whirl up to my gate
Crested silvery white !

THE DUCK'S VOICE

Night over the sea
Is falling and wild ducks' cries
Are trailing whitely.

Akikaze no
Fukedo mo aoki
Kuri no iga
    Bashō (1644–1694)

Meigetsu ya
Mon ni sashi-kuru
Shio gashira
    Bashō

Umi kurete
Kamo no koe
Honoka ni shiroshi
    Bashō

BUTTERFLY

When the breeze goes by,
Each time upon the willow
Shifts the butterfly.

CRICKET

Ah, alas, ah how
Heartless : beneath the helmet
Chirps the cricket now !

LESPEDEZAS

Stem by slender stem
Lespedezas sway but drop
Not white dews from them.

Fukutabini
Chō no inaoru
Yanagi kana
Bashō

Muzanna ya
Kabuto no shita no
Kirigirisu
Bashō

Shiratsuyu wo
Kobosanu hagi no
Unerikana
Bashō

MOON AND PLUM

With the moon and sweet
Plum-blossoms, the scene of spring
Is almost complete.

CUCKOO'S VOICE

Cuckoo's voice above,
The moon is gleaming brightly
Through great bamboo-grove.

THE HARVEST MOON

Harvest moon is bright:
Around the lake we tarry
All through the long night.

Haru mo haya	Hototogisu	Meigetsu ya
Keshiki totonou	O-takeyabu wo	Ike wo megurite
Tsuki to ume	Moru tsuki-yo	Yomosugara
Bashō (1644–1694)	*Bashō*	*Bashō*

THE SHINING HALL

Oh, the Shining Hall
In the heavy May-rain is
Left untouched by all !

SPRING NIGHT

While we viewed the gay
Blossoms of the cherry-trees,
Spring night passed away.

SPRING MORNING

Season of spring days !
There a nameless hill has veils
Of soft morning haze.

Samidare no
Furi nokoshite ya
Hikarido
Bashō

Haru no yowa
Sakura ni akete
Shimai keri
Bashō

Harunare ya
Namo naki yama no
Asagasumi
Bashō

AUTUMN EVENING

None is traveling
Here along this way but I, —
This autumn evening.

SAGA BAMBOO

(For a picture)

How refreshing there
Seems the Saga bamboo-grove ! —
A picture of cool air.

THE HIBISCUS BRANCH

At the road-side, fair
Hibiscus branch was eaten
By my riding mare.

Kono michi ya
Yuku-hito nashi ni
Aki no kure
    Bashō (1644–1694)

Suzushisa wo
E ni utsushi keri
Saga no take
    Bashō

Michinobe no
Mokuge wa uma ni
Kuraware keri
    Bashō

CAMELLIA FLOWER

Fair camellia-bell
Spilled the shining drops of clear
Water as it fell.

THE LAST VERSE

Having become ill
This journey, o'er withered moors
My dream wanders still.

THE EIGHT VIEWS OF ŌMI

*(On being requested to compose a poem containing
eight famous views of Lake Lute at Ōmi)*

Seven views are well
Hidden in the mist, but I
Hear the Mii's bell.

Ochizama ni
Mizu koboshi keri
Hanatsubaki
   Bashō

Tabi ni yande
Yume wa kareno wo
Kake meguru
   Bashō

Shichi kei wa
Kiri ni kakurete
Mii no kane
   Bashō (?)

17

THE CHANGE OF GARMENT

At the change to sheer
Garments, into the "long-chest"
Spring will disappear.

LATE SPRING

Pale, the yellow rose
In spring already — bitter,
Too, the lettuce grows.

SNOWY HERON

In the vernal breeze
How snowy is the heron
Flying through pine-trees.

Nagamochi ni
Haru zo kureyuku
Koromogae
Saikaku
(1641–1693)

Haru mo haya
Yamabuki shiroku
Chisa nigashi
Sodō (1641–1716)

Harukaze ya
Shirasagi shiroshi
Matsu no naka
Raizan
(1653–1716)

18

AT SAGA

How sad : a holy
Nun stands mid insects' singing
So melancholy !

WINTER GALE

Winter gale that raves
Dies away till it remains
As the roar of waves.

FIREFLIES

(*At the age of Seven*)

Even though I say,
"Come to me, O, come to me,"
Fireflies go away.

Asamashi ya
Mushi naku naka ni
Ama hitori
    Raizan

Kogarashi no
Hate wa arikeri
Umi no oto
    Gonsui
        (1649–1722)

Koi koi to
Iedo hotaru ga
Tonde yuku
    Onitsura
        (1660–1738)

BATH-WATER

Insects singing their lay,
Not a place find I to throw
Bath-water away !

THE CHANGE OF GARMENT

As I change to sheer
Garments, even I rejoice
With no loved one here.

AUTUMN MOON

On the moon tonight
I wonder if there can be
Any who won't write !

Gyosui no
Sute dokoro nashi
Mushi no koe
  Onitsura
    (1660–1738)

Koi mo nai
Mi ni mo ureshi ya
Koromogae
  Onitsura

Fude toranu
Hito mo arōka
Kyō no tsuki
  Onitsura

20

HARVEST MOON

Harvest moon is bright,
Casting the shadows of pine
On the mats tonight!

CHERRY–SPRAYS

Before giving me
The note, the messenger holds out
Sprays of cherry-tree.

THE BELL IN WINTER RAIN

"Hark!" seems the refrain
From the bell that comes at night
With the wintery rain.

Meigetsu ya
Tatami no ue ni
Matsu no kage
     Kikaku
          (1660–1707)

Fumi wa ato ni
Sakura sashidasu
Tsukai kana
     Kikaku

Are kike to
Shigure kuru yo no
Kane no koe
     Kikaku

EARLY SPRING

Warm the weather grows
Gradually as one plum-flower
After another blows.

HARVEST MOON

Harvest moon on high
Paints the aged pine against
The deepening blue sky.

NEW YEAR'S DAY

On the New Year's Day
The sky has cleared and sparrows
Chatter bright and gay.

Ume ichirin
Ichirin hodo no
Atatakasa
    Ransetsu
        (1653–1707)

Aozora ni
Matsu wo kaitari
Kyō no tsuki
    Ransetsu

Ganjitsu ya
Harete suzume no
Monogatari
    Ransetsu

22

HARVEST MOON

Harvest moon rose bright
Over the water where crept
Vapors, silvery white !

DEWS

Play about, O, fair
Beads of dew, from one grass-leaf
To another there !

AUTUMN CICADA

Ah, alas, beside
Its shell an autumn cicada
Lies just as it died !

Meigetsu ya
Kemuri hai-yuku
Mizu no ue
   Ransetsu

Kusa no ha wo
Asobi arike yo
Tsuyu no tama
   Ransetsu

Nukegara to
Narabite shinuru
Aki no semi
   Jōsō (1661–1704)

23

NIGHTINGALE

There the nightingale
Sings at moon-remaining dawn
In the tea-plant dale.

ON PARTING FROM MY OLD
MASTER BELOW A SLOPE

Eating persimmon
We look up the sloping hill
Ere we part alone.

CRICKETS

Crickets sing so sweet
Into windows left unfinished
With the paper-sheet.

Uguisu ya
Chanoki batake no
Asa zukiyo
   Sōjo (17th Cent.)

Wakaruru ya
Kaki kuinagara
Oka no ue
   Izen (16?–1710)

Harinokosu
Mado ni naki iru
Itodo kana
   Izen

WINTER GALE

Whirling all around,
Winter gale doesn't let bleak rain
Drop upon the ground.

SUMMER HEAT

Stones and trees that meet
My eyes glare straight at me
In the intense heat.

FIREFLY

(*On the death of my younger sister Chine*)

Pitifully upon
My palm the little firefly
Has perished alone !

Kogarashi no
Chini mo otosanu
Shigure kana
   Kyorai
      (1651–1704)

Ishi mo ki mo
Manako ni hikaru
Atsusakana
   Kyorai

Te no ue ni
Kanashiku kiyuru
Hotaru kana
   Kyorai

25

MAPLE–LEAVES

Autumn brings the cold
Rain already on the crags,
Maple with first gold.

RAPE–FLOWERS

There a castle towers
So high at Kōriyama
Mid the gold rape-flowers.

WEED

Though I do not know
Their names, each weed has lovely
Flowers that sweetly blow.

Aki mo haya
Iwa ni shigurete
Hatsu momiji
Kyoroku
(1655–1715)

Na no haha no
Naka ni shiro ari
Kōriyama
Kyoroku

Nawashirazu
Kusa goto ni hana
Aware nari
Sampū
(1646–1732)

26

THE LITTLE FROGS

At my cottage-door
The little frogs are swimming
In May-rain's downpour !

MAPLE LEAVES

Envied by us all,
The leaves of maple turn so
Beautiful — then fall !

THE SNIPES

The snipes rise in flight
From the voice that scolds the cow
In the soft twilight.

Samidare ni
Kawazu no oyogu
Toguchi kana
Sampū

Urayamashi
Utsukushū natte
Chiru momiji
Shikō (1664–1731)

Ushi shikaru
Koe ni shigi tatsu
Yū-be kana
Shikō

FLOWERY DALE

Narrowly a trail
Fades away into the dusk
In the flowery dale.

INSECTS' SONG

Toward insects' song
Narrower becomes the pass
As it winds along.

THE NEW YEAR'S GREETING

Chōmatsu came
To say the New Year's Greeting
In his parent's name.

Michisuji no	Mushi no ne ni	Chōmatsu ga
Hosō kietaru	Semamatte yuku	Oya no na de kuru
Hana no kana	Yamaji kana	Gyokei kana
Fukoku	*Fukoku*	*Yaha* (1662–1740)
(17th Cent.)		

VIOLETS

Violets abound
Within the rigid fences
Of prohibited ground !

CAMELLIA FLOWERS

After I swept all
Over the garden, blossoms
Of a camellia fall.

THE CHERRY-TREE

(After his hut is burnt down)

I am burnt out but
The cherries had their glory
At this very hut !

Hattoba no
Kaki yori uchi wa
Sumire kana
Yaha

Haki sōji
Shitekara tsubaki
Chirini-keri
Yaha

Yakeni keri
Saredomo hana wa
Chiri sumashi
Hokushi
(16?–1718)

29

THE FIREFLY

In the lonely night
There the firefly glides one foot,
Putting out its light.

POET'S FANCY

Covered with the flowers,
Instantly I'd like to die
In this dream of ours!

THE SHRIKE

The shrike cries above
When the sunset's mellow rays
Flood the red-pine grove.

Sabishisa ya
Isshaku kie-te
Tobu hotaru
Hokushi
    (16?–1718)

Hana ni umarete
Yumeyori sugu ni
Shinan kana
Etsujin
    (16?–1702)

Mozu naku ya
Irihi sashi komu
Mematsubara
Bonchō
    (16?–1714)

MAPLE LEAVES

Cutting bamboos, cold
Is the hill of maple leaves
Half-russet and gold.

NIGHT—RAIN

At the lower Kyō,
The night-rain falls so softly
On the fallen snow.

BRIGHT MOON

Bright moon in the sky
Is a comrade for the bleak
Gale that hurries by.

Hadasamushi
Take kiru yama no
Usu momiji
  Bonchō

Shimo Kyō ya
Yuki tsumu ue no
Yoru no ame
  Bonchō

Fukukaze no
Aiet ya sora ni
Tsuki hitotsu
  Bonchō

31

AUTUMN SKY

Drifting clouds, on high
And below, pass each other
In the autumn sky.

THE RIVER

See a river flow
In a long and tedious line
On the field of snow.

THE SCARECROW

What a lonely sound —
Ah, alone the scarecrow falls
Down along the ground !

Ue yuku to
Shita kuru kumoya
Aki no sora
Bonchō
(16?–1714)

Naganaga to
Kawa hitosuji ya
Yuki no hara
Bonchō

Mono no oto
Hitori taoruru
Kagashi kana
Bonchō

A CHILLY NIGHT

Few times in the chill
Of the night changes the sound
Of the rapid rill.

FIREFLY

Cold I feel as I
Grasp the needles of the pine
With a firefly.

WHITE CHRYSANTHEMUMS

Having seen the sight
Of all chrysanthemums, my eyes
Come back to the white.

Se no oto no
Nisando kawaru
Yozamu kana
   Rôkwa
      (1669–1703)

Matsu no ha wo
Tsumetô nigiru
Hotaru kana
   Rôkwa

Mitsukushita
Mewa shiragiku ni
Modori keri
   Isshô (1652–1688)

CHERRY-FLOWERS

Cherries are so fair :
In full bloom behind the great
Buddha's image there.

SPRING MORNING

From the long hallways
Voices of the people rise
In the morning haze.

RAPE-FIELD

In the rape-field how
Sad the insects' voices sound
Mid the late shoots now !

Daibutsu no
Ushiro ni hana no
Sakari kana
    Rotsu (1716–1736)

Asagiri ya
Rōka ni noboru
Hito no koe
    Ryōto (1660–1717)

Nabatake ya
Futaha no naka no
Mushi no koe
    Shōhaku
      (1649–1722)

IN AUTUMN

Autumn wind blows cold
Through the pines and firs upon
Battlefields of old.

CRESCENT MOON

'Neath the crescent moon
Silver dews upon the grass
Chill my hand so soon !

SEA–LICE

Underneath the bright
Harvest moon, the sea-lice run
On the stone tonight.

Matsu sugi no
Akikaze samushi
Kosenjō
   Tōrin (1638–1719)

Mikazuki ya
Haya te ni sawaru
Kusa no tsuyu
   Tōrin

Meigetsu ya
Funamushi hashiru
Ishi no ue
   Tōrin

CAMELLIA FLOWER

Oh, camellia-bell
Comes up at dawn in the wooden
Bucket from the well!

IN THE MOOR-LAND

In the moor-land I
Worshipped the Buddha in lightning
As it flashed by.

SPEARMEN

In the drizzling, drear
Shower, still higher the spearmen
Lift each gilded spear.

Akebono no
Tsurube ni agaru
Tsubaki kana
    Kakei (16?–1716)

Inazuma ni
Daibutsu ogamu
Nonaka kana
    Kakei

Yarimochi no
Naho furi tatsuru
Shigure kana
    Masahide
        (1655–1723)

HARVEST MOON

What a fair and bright
Harvest moon ! there may be some
Babies born tonight !

AUTUMN TEMPEST

Autumn tempest raves,
Roars, and rages, and at last
Runs o'er ocean-waves.

WINTER NIGHT

In the frosty night
Not a hue upon the things
Stirs before the sight.

Meigetsu ya
Koyoi umaruru
Ko mo aran
    Shintoku
        (1632–1698)

Arearete
Sue wa umi yuku
Nowaki kana
    Ensui (1639–1704)

Hitoiro mo
Ugoku mono naki
Shimo no yoru
    Yasui (1657–1743)

IN AUTUMN

Oh, how bright and gay !
Departing autumn scatters
Maples on its way.

AUTUMN BUTTERFLY

Autumn butterflies
Don't be blown against the pine
By the gust of breeze.

INSECTS' VOICE

Through the sounds of drear
Tempest blowing shingles off,
Insects' voice I hear.

Yuku aki no
Michimichi kobosu
Momiji kana
   Otsuyū
     (1674–1739)

Matsu no ki ni
Fuki aterarena
Aki no chō
   Shūsen
     (1653–1737)

Yane makuru
Bōfū no naka ya
Mishi no koe
   Riyū (1660–1705)

SPRING MOON

The spring moon is bright;
Many ask me what I am
Looking at this night!

LOTUS–SEEDS

In the silent air
Many a time the lotus-seeds
Fly out on the mere.

WINTER MOOR

In the withered moor
Voices scolding at the horse
Are also storm's roar.

Nani miruto
Tou hito ōshi
Haru no tsuki
  Bakusui
      (1720–1783)

Shizukesa ya
Hasu no mi no tobu
Amatatabi
  Bakusui

Uma shikaru
Koe mo kareno no
Arashi kana
  Kyokusui
      (16?–1719)

DRIZZLING RAINS

Showering horses, run
Drizzling rains but leaving cows
In the setting sun.

WEEPING WILLOWS

In the heart of town
Willows growing at the inn
Bend their branches down.

HEAT–WAVES

Where the heat-waves play,
Softly rustles down the sand
From the bank near by.

Uma nurete
Ushi wa yūhi no
Murashigure
    Tokoku

Machi naka e
Shidaruru yado no
Yanagi kana
    Rigyu

Kagerō ya
Horohoro ochiru
Kishi no suna
    Doho

FIREFLIES

Ah, the lost child cries
And cries, but still he catches
Many fireflies !

HARVEST MOON

In an ecstasy
'Neath the harvest moon a verse
Flashes into me.

SKYLARK

Singing clear and loud,
A skylark makes the silver
Ripples on the cloud.

Mayoi go no
Nakunaku tsukamu
Hotaru kana
   Ryusui
     (1691–1758)

Meigetsu ya
Kotsuzen to shite
Ikku kana
   Sekkei

Kumo ni nami
Tatete saezuru
Hibari kana
   Seien

THE HAZE

Far above the veil
Of the haze a boat, at times,
Rises with its sail.

PICTURE PRINT

Blooming coxcomb-plant
Is taller than the wall where
Prints are dried aslant.

CRIMSON PLUM FLOWERS

Green new bamboo-flume
Runs athwart against the sweet
Crimson plums in bloom.

Kasumi yori	Sōshi hosu	Kōbai ni
Tokidoki amaru	Kabe yori takashi	Awoku yokotō
Hokakebune	Hageitō	Kakehi kana
Gakoku	*Tantan*	*Hyōsui*
(1639–1710)	(1675–1761)	(1678–1755)

RED MAPLE–LEAVES

Inky clouds sun cleaves
And suddenly it flashes
On red maple-leaves.

WHEAT FIELD

The spring breeze is sweet
As it blows with sounds of stream
Murmuring through the wheat.

THE GAD–FLY

On the screen a gray
Shadow of gad-fly alights,
Indian summer day.

Kurokumo ni
Katto hi no sasu
Momiji kana
    Mokudō

Harukaze ya
Mugi no naka yuku
Mizu no oto
    Mokudō

Abu no kage
Shōji ni utsuru
Koharu kana
    Yayū (1701–1783)

43

THE CUCKOO

If the cuckoo were
Lovely blossoms I would pluck
One sweet note from her !

THE CHERRY BLOSSOMS
OF MT. YOSHINO

Clad in cherry-bloom
Mt. Yoshino hides itself,
Flower in flowery brume.

HARVEST MOON AND INSECTS

Brightly shines the moon:
Where the silver shadows are,
Insects string their tune.

Hana naraba	Hana ni hana	Meigetsu ya
Hitokoe oramu	Kakure-te hana no	Kuraki tokoro wa
Hototogisu	Yoshinoyama	Mushi no koe
Kodo (?–1738)	*Tōfu*	*Bunson*
		(16?–1713)

44

THE MORNING–GLORY

Gift-water, I pray,
The morning-glory has taken
Well-bucket away.

THE CUCKOO

While upon my theme
I pondered "Cuckoo, cuckoo" —
Day has dawned with gleam !

LONGING FOR
A DEPARTED CHILD

I wonder where may
My small dragonfly-hunter
Be wandering today !

Asagao ni	Hototogisu	Tonbo tsuri
Tsurube torarete	Hototogisu tote	Kyō wa doko made
Morai mizu	Akeni keri	Itta yara
Chiyo (1701–1775)	*Chiyo*	*Chiyo*

WHITE CHRYSANTHEMUM

Look: O how gruesome
Are rouged finger-nails against
White Chrysanthemum !

PLUM-BLOSSOM

(*Good for Evil*)

Flowers give their perfume
To the one who breaks the branch
From the plum in bloom.

IN PENSIVE MOOD

I sit, I lie, yet
How spacious seems the linen-
Gauze-mosquito-net.

Shiragiku ya
Benisaita te no
Osoroshiki
   Chiyo (1701–1775)

Taoraruru
Hito ni kaoru ya
Ume no hana
   Chiyo

Okite mitsu
Nete mitsu kaya no
Hirosakana
   Ukihashi

CHERRY-TREE

Drunken fellow, be
Careful 'bout the blossoming
Well-side cherry-tree !

SNOWY MORNING

Tracks of clogs I found
On snowy morn like figure
"Two" upon the ground.

AFTER MY HUT IS
BURNT DOWN

On my ruins, fair
Flowers of violet are now
Blowing here and there !

Idobata no
Sakura abunashi
Sake no yoi
   Shūshiki
       (1668–1725)

Yuki no asa
Ninoji ninoji no
Geta no ato
   Sute-Jo
       (1633–1698)

Yakeshi no ne
Tokoro dokoro ya
Sumiregusa
   Shokyū-Ni
       (1713–1781)

NIGHTINGALES

The nightingales sing
In the echo of the bell
Tolled at evening.

RUDDUCK

On the crags I hear
The rudduck's singing voices
Rolling high and clear.

GRASSHOPPERS

In the rugged, torn
Scarecrow's sleeves grasshoppers are
Chirping so forlorn !

Iriai no
Hibiki no naka ya
Hototogisu
    Ukō

Komadori no
Koe korobi keri
Iwa no ue
    Sono-Jo
      (1649–1723)

Kirigirisu
Naku ya kagashi no
Sode no naka
    Chigetsu-Ni
      (1632–1706)

48

SPRING RAIN

Oh, the rains of spring,
An umbrella and raincoat
Pass by, conversing.

CAMELLIA-FLOWER

Fair camellia-flower,
As it drops, spills the water
From the yester-shower.

THE PEONY

Scattered, the peony:
One beside the other pile,
Petals two or three.

Harusame ya
Monogatari yuku
Mi no to kasa
Buson (1715–1783)

Tsubaki chitte
Kinyō no ame wo
Koboshi keri
Buson

Botan chitte
. Uchi-kasanarinu
Ni san pen
Buson

49

BUTTERFLY

Lit upon the bell
Of the temple, a butterfly
Is sleeping so well.

THE CASTLE

Oh, how challenging
Is the castle on the cliff,
Wrapped with leaves of spring!

IN LATE SPRING

Young court maid, you send
No replying ode to me!
Spring is at its end.

Tsurigane ni
Tomarite nemuru
Kochō kana
    Buson (1715–1783)

Zetchō no
Shiro tanomoshiki
Wakaba kana
    Buson

Henka naki
Ao-nyōbō yo
Haru no kure
    Buson

IN SPRING

All day long the spring
Ocean is undulating
And undulating.

MAY–RAIN

In the rain of May
Two cottages border the river
Flowing on her way.

FULLING–MALLET

Here and there I hear
The sound of fulling-mallet
Beating soft and clear.

Haru no umi
Hinemosu notari
Notari kana
Buson

Samidare ya
Ōkawa wo mae ni
Ie niken
Buson

Ochi kochi
Ochi kochi to utsu
Kinuta kana
Buson

FIREFLIES

What joy it is to let
Fireflies loose within the linen-
Gauze-mosquito-net !

CHILLY NIGHT

In a chilly night
A thief has vanished away
On the roof in fright.

AT MT. YOSHINO

At Yoshino there
Is no thief of cherry-flowers
Blowing wild and fair !

Kaya no uchi ni
Hotaru hanashi-te
Aa ureshi ya
    Buson (1715–1783)

Nusubito no
Yane ni kieyuku
Yozamu kana
    Buson

Mi-yoshino ni
Hana nusubito wa
Nakari keri
    Buson

AUTUMN–TWILIGHT

The hills cast shadows
And pampas-grass is swaying
In sunset meadows.

THE TEMPLE BELL

Cool, how cool they are :
Voices of the bell depart
From the bell afar.

IN WINTER

Willow-trees are bare —
Dried the water, and the stones
Lying here and there.

Yama wa kure	Suzushisa ya	Yanagi chiri
No wa tasogare no	Kane wo hanaruru	Mizu kare ishi
Suzuki kana	Kane no koe	Tokoro dokoro
Buson	*Buson*	*Buson*

AUTUMN EVE

When alone I leave
The gate I too am a wanderer
In this autumn eve.

CHERRY-FLOWERS

On the pass where we
Tread on clouds, there in the rain
Blows the cherry-tree.

SEAWEED

Seaweed's taste and scent
Are what was left by water
In the reef's soft dent.

Mon wo izureba	Kumo wo fumu	Aonori ya
Ware mo yukuhito	Yamaji ni ame no	Ishi no kubomi no
Aki no kure	Sakura kana	Wasure zio
Buson	*Kito* (1740–1789)	*Kito*

THE SCARECROW

The scarecrow's shadow
Leans out to the road along
The sunset meadow.

ENJOYING THE COOL

Ah, the beautiful
Woman dries her hair in dusk,
Enjoying the cool !

SCORCHED PLAIN

From behind the rain
Comes with swift pursuing steps
Across the scorched plain.

Yū-hi kage
Michimade izuru
Kagashi kana
   Shōha (?–1771)

Suzumi ite
Yami ni kamihosu
Onna kana
   Shōha

Ushiro yori
Ame no oikuru
Yakeno kana
   Tairō (?–1778)

55

PEONY FLOWER

Now, how dear to me
Is my father's rage when I
Broke the peony.

UGUISU (NIGHTINGALE)

Smooth and round and long
Is the voice of uguisu
Singing its sweet song.

PATRINIA FLOWER

There is one big stone
Beside a sweet patrinia
Blossoming alone.

Botan orishi
Chichi no ikari zo
Natsukashiki
　Tairō (?–1778)

Uguisu no
Koe namerakani
Maruku nagashi
　Tōkō (1752–1819)

Katawara ni
Ōki na ishi ya
Ominaeshi
　Gekkyo
　　(1745–1824)

56

WINTER MOON

Winter moon on high,
Naught was heard but the clogs' sound
As on the bridge pass I.

A BEE

With a buzzing cry
A bee changes blossom sought
By a butterfly.

THE SNOW

How serene and so
Beautiful the day becomes
On the fallen snow !

Kangetsu ya
Ware hitori yuku
Hashi no ue
   Taigi (1709–1772)

Koetatete
Inaoru hachi ya
Hana no chō
   Taigi

Utsukushiki
Hiyori ni narinu
Yuki no ue
   Taigi

GARDEN PLUM

"Don't you break," said he
And saying, broke the garden
Plum and gave to me.

FIREFLIES

"Look, O look, there fly
Fireflies," I would like to say —
But alone am I.

HARVEST MOON

Harvest moon is bright,
Rising from the windy grass
Of the moor tonight!

Naori zo to
Orite kure keri
Sono no ume
   Taigi (1709–1772)

Tobu hotaru
Are to yuwan mo
Hitori kana
   Taigi

Arashi fuku
Kusa no nakayori
Kyō no tsuki
   Chōra
     (1729–1781)

WILD GEESE

There the wild geese file
And sink behind the high ridge
Of the sunset hill.

PLUM-FLOWERS

As I put on the light,
More plum-flowers are seen behind
Branches fair and white.

IN AUTUMN

Wind has mournful tune,
And alas, night after night
Wanes the autumn moon.

Karigane no	Hitomose ba	Kaze kanashi
Kasanari ochiru	Uraume gachi ni	Yo yo ni kageyuku
Yamabe kana	Miyuru nari	Tsuki no kage
Chōra	*Gyōdai*	*Gyōdai*

(1732-1793)

59

THE RIVER OF HEAVEN

Far above the bright
Stars the River of Heaven
Seems to flow tonight !

SPRING EVENING

How I long for one :
When the light begins to shine
Cherries fall alone.

GENTLE WILLOW

Came home angrily,
I found within my garden
Gentle willow-tree.

Ama no kawa
Hoshi yori ue ni
Miyuru kana
  Shirao
      (1735-1792)

Hito koishi
Hitomosu koro wo
Sakura chiru
  Shirao

Muttoshi-te
Modoreba niwa ni
Yanagi kana
  Ryōta (1707-1787)

CHERRY-TREE

While we did not see
This world for a near three days
Blows the cherry-tree.

WINTER NIGHT

Night advances on :
Sounds of breaking charcoal with
Charcoal are heard alone.

VISITOR

In the moonlit night
A man calls at my cottage,
I put on the light.

Yo no naka wa	Fukeru yo ya	Hito no kite
Mikka minuma ni	Sumi mote sumi wo	Hitomosu tsuki no
Sakura kana	Kudaku oto	Iori kana
Ryōta	*Ryōta*	*Chodō*

(1748–1814)

IN WINTER

Breaking off each day
Withered river-rushes go
Drifting on their way.

SUMMER NIGHT

Swiftly runs the bright
Moon from cloud to cloud on high
In a summer night.

NEW YEAR'S DAY

On the New Year's Day
How calm is Mount Higashi's
Pine-trees in array !

Kare ashi no
Hi ni hi ni orete
Nagare keri
   Rankō(1726–1799)

Natsu no yo ya
Kumo yori kumo ni
Tsuki hashiru
   Rankō

Ganjitsu ya
Matsu shizuka naru
Higashiyama
   Rankō

COXCOMB'S BLOOM

There the coxcomb's bloom
Has nothing of the autumn's
Melancholy gloom.

ORPHAN SPARROW

With one another
Let's play, so come, O sparrow
Who has no mother.

POOR FLIES

Oh, no, do not beat
Them, — these flies who wring their hands
And who wring their feet.

Keitō ni
Aki no aware wa
Nakari-keri
  Rankō

Wareto kite
Asobe ya oya no
Nai suzume
  Issa (1763–1827)

Yare utsu na
Haiga te wo suru
Ashi wo suru
  Issa

THE CHERRY BLOSSOMS
AT UENO

Underneath the fair
Blossoms of the cherry-tree
None are strangers there.

A NAP

I would take a nice
Nap at noon letting the hill's
Streamlet pound my rice.

LIVING IN THE TOWN

Living in the town
One must have money even
To melt the snow down !

Hana no kage
Aka no tanin wa
Nakari keri
   Issa (1763–1827)

Sansui ni
Kome wo tsukashite
Hirune kana
   Issa

Machi sumai ya
Yuki wo tokasu mo
Kane ga iru
   Issa

YEAR'S END

With the wings, O, here
And there, money is flying
At the end of the year.

A RADISH-WORKER

With the radish he
Pulled out, a radish-worker
Shows the road for me.

THE NEW YEAR'S DREAM

I am full of tear
Seeing my home in the first
Dream of the New Year.

Hane hae-te
Kane ga tobunari
Toshi no **kure**
  Issa

Daiko hiki
Daiko de michi wo
Oshie keri
  Issa

Hatsu-yume ya
Furusato wo mite
Namida kana
  Issa

65

LITTLE ONE

Begging for the bright
Harvest moon, how loudly cries
Little one at night !

INSECTS

If you think they do
Naught but cry and cry, maybe
Insects laugh at you.

FROST

Biting frost, O, come
As you please : there is no flower
After chrysanthemum.

Meigetsu wo
Totte kurero to
Naku ko kana
   Issa (1763–1827)

Nakuto bakari
Kikanaba mushi no
Warou beshi
   Ōemaru
     (1719–1805)

Oke ya shimo
Kiku yori hana wa
Hana mo nashi
   Ōemaru

TEMPLE BELL

Oh, how still ! the boom
Of the temple bell does not
Stir the cherry-bloom.

DAYBREAK

At the daybreak, oh,
The raging storm is buried
In the heavy snow !

THE MILKY WAY

The Milky Way looks near
As though easily I could jump
Over it from here !

Shizukasa ya
Hana ni sawaranu
Kane no koe
   Fuhaku
     (1714–1807)

Akebono ya
Arashi wa yuki ni
Uzumore-te
   Shirō (1742–1813)

Ama no kawa
Tobikosu hodo ni
Miyuru kana
   Shirō

WATERFALL

Down into the lush
Foliage drops the waterfall
With its thundering crush.

NEW YEAR'S DAY

Ah, the New Year's Day
At my humble cottage door,
Too, has passed away !

A HAZY DAYBREAK

What a daybreak, oh,
And in addition — haze
To the moon and snow !

Tō tō to	Ganjitsu mo	Tsuki yuki no
Taki no ochikomu	Sugiyuku kusa no	Hoka ni kasumi no
Shigemi kana	Tobira kana	Asaborake
Shirō (1742–1813)	*Seibi* (1748–1816)	*Michihiko*
		(1755–1818)

FIREFLIES

Fireflies, as they gleam,
Float together with the weed
On a gentle stream.

AUTUMN EVENING

From my hut's doorway
One's shadow is cast at the close
Of an autumn day.

AT ISHIYAMA

Right and left of me
At Ishiyama, fireflies
And the moon I see.

Ukikusa to
Tomo ni nagareru
Ho taru kana
  Ginko

Toguchi yori
Hitokage sashinu
Aki no kure
  Seira

Ishiyama ya
Tsukito hotaru to
Migi hidari
  Koyū-Ni

CHRYSANTHEMUMS

Ah, into one shade
Many-hued chrysanthemums
Wither, die, and fade !

A SILVER-EYE

Following my high
Whistle on the mountain road
Comes a silver-eye.

PHEASANT

Pheasant flaps the wings
Suddenly at eve and I
Broke the koto-strings.

Iroiro no
Kiku hitoiro ni
Kare ni keri
Ryusui

Kuchibue ni
Mejiro tsuki kuru
Yamaji kana
Sogetsu-Ni
(?-1804)

Kiji ha utte
Koto no o kireshi
Yube kana
Seifu-Ni
(1731-1814)

PLUM AND A MOON

On the plum in flower
By my eave, the pale moon hangs
At the dawning hour.

NIGHT–FAIR

Plums are falling white
Where household marts are open
At Osaka-night.

NIGHTINGALES

Nightingales flee, but
Still I hear the singing voice
High above my hut.

Noki no ume	Umechiru ya	Hototogisu
Tsuki ni yoake no	Naniwa no yoru no	Nigete mo nigete mo
Kakari-keri	Dōgu-ichi	An no sora
Tenro	*Kyucho*	*Soheki*

WINTER NIGHT

Underneath the bright
Winter moon I met a tall
Buddhist priest at night.

SEAWEED

Seaweed's scent is keen :
Shadows of two priests are cast
On the paper screen.

IN LATE FALL

The autumn passes
Yet there are sparrows hopping
Among the grasses.

Se no takaki	Nori no ka ya	Yuku aki ya
Hōshi ni ainu	Shōji ni utusuru	Suzume no ariku
Fuyu no tsuki	Sō futari	Kusa no naka
Baishitsu	*Baishitsu*	*Sōkyū* (1760–1843)
(1768–1852)		

THE MIST

I turned back to see
But the man I passed was veiled
In mist already.

THE BANANA-PLANT

Light reflects aslant
From my neighbor on the leaves
Of the banana-plant.

WILD GEESE

Wild geese take a flight
Low along the railroad tracks
In the moonlit night.

Kaeri mireba
Yukiaishi hito
Kasumi-keri
   Shiki (1866–1902)

Tonari kara
Tomoshi no utsuru
Bashō kana
   Shiki

Kishiyamichi ni
Hikuku gan tobu
Tsukiyo kana
   Shiki

73

IN SPRING

What a perfumed breeze !
A temple 'mid the thousand
Hills of verdant trees.

ON THE WITHERED PLAIN

There the gates remain
Alone at Buddhist temple
On the withered plain.

FIRECRACKERS

O, how bright and gay
Bloom firecrackers o'er the high
Tree-tops far away.

Gunpū ya	Mon bakari	Ki no sue ni
Senzan no midori	Nokoru kareno no	Toku no hanabi
Tera hitotsu	Garan kana	Hiraki-keri
Shiki (1866–1902)	*Shiki*	*Shiki*

74

WINTER SUNSET

Winter sun has set
But how clear the castle's pines
'Gainst the blue as yet !

THE CRESCENT MOON

Rolling waves as they
Toss, whirl up the crescent moon,
Then recede away.

SUMMER MOON

Underneath the bright
Summer moon many lay down
On the deck at night.

Fuyu no hi no
Ochite akarushi
Shiro no matsu
  Shiki

Aranami ya
Futsuka no tsuki wo
Maite saru
  Shiki

Kappan ni
Neruhito ōshi
Natsu no tsuki
  Shiki

THE THISTLE-FLOWERS

Delicate and fine
Purple is the thistle-flower
But with many a spine !

THE OCEAN MOON

From the distant bound
Of the cool, the ocean moon
Rises bright and round.

YELLOW ROSES

Yellow roses blow
Beside the clay-dolls drying
On the mat of straw.

Murasaki no	Suzushisa no	Yamabuki ya
Hana no toge aru	Hateyori detaru	Ningyo kawaku
Azami kana	Umi no tsuki	Hito mushiro
Shiki (1866–1902)	*Shiki*	*Shiki*

GOLDEN MAPLE-SPRAY

City folks are they :
In the home-bound train they hold
Golden maple-spray.

NEW YEAR'S DAY

It's the New Year's Day :
Unbroken line of Emperor —
Fuji in array !

A BUTTERFLY

To the wreaths that lie
Sweetly on the casket-lid,
Comes a butterfly.

Kyō bito ya
Momiji kazashite
Modori gisha
   Meisetsu
      (1847–1925)

Ganjitsu ya
Ikkei no tenshi
Fuji no yama
   Meisetsu

Chō chō no
Shitou hanawa ya
Kan no ue
   Meisetsu

BUTTERFLIES

Of their dreams on gay
Flowers I'd ask the butterflies,
But no voice have they.

HARVEST MOON

Underneath the moon
Of autumn, my neighbor plays
A flute out of tune.

LEAVES

Leaves, O, ask the breeze
Which of you will scatter first
From the verdant trees?

Hana no yume
Kikitaki chō ni
Koe mo nashi
Reikan

Meigetsu ni
Mazui fue fuku
Tonari kana
Kōyō (1886–1903)

Kaze ni kike
Izure ga saki ni
Chiru konoha
Sōseki (1865–1915)

TRAIN

Following up the train,
The long black smoke is crawling
O'er the withered plain.

SNOWY MORNING

Opening the door
I am so surprised at morn
With the snow all o'er !

ON DEATH OF MADAME OTSUKA

Throw into the tomb
All of the lovely blossoms
Of chrysanthemum.

Kisha o otte
Kemuri hai yuku
Kareno kana
   Sōseki

To wo akete
Odoroku yuki no
Ashita kana
   Sōseki

Aruhodo no
Kiku nage-ire yo
Kan no naka
   Sōseki

SPRING DAY

(On parting from Kyoshi during my stay at Matsuyama)

What a long spring day !
Catching yawns from one another
We go each our way.

A BEE

Many a time the bee
Stung the Buddha made of stone,
Very angrily !

OLD FORT

Even now, O, there
Remains the fort: wisterias
Blooming sweet and fair.

Nagaki hi ya
Akubi utsushite
Wakare yuku
   Sōseki (1865–1915)

Hachi gekishite
Sekibutsu wo sasu
Amatatabi
   Bakusui
     (1873–1913)

Mushaotoshi
Ima ni nokorite
Fuji no hana
   Otsuji (1881–1919)

SHOWER

Shower comes but passes,
Leaving the bright summer moon
Upon the grasses.

HARVEST MOON

Underneath the bright
Harvest moon even my horse
Likes the road tonight.

NEW YEAR'S MORN

Purple, white, and lo :
It becomes the New Year's morn
On the fallen snow.

Yūdachi no
Nokoshite yukinu
Kusa no tsuki
   Shō-u (1860–   )

Kyō no tsuki
Uma mo yomichi wo
Konomi keri
   Kijō (1870–1935)

Shira jira to
Kotoshi ni narinu
Yuki no ue
   Shō-u

CHILLY NIGHT

I pursue the light
Of the swift-footed lantern
In the chilly night.

AUTUMN WIND

When the autumn wind
Blows there is but haiku
In all things I find.

THE WITHERING MOOR

Sun is shining o'er
The distant mountains across
The withering moor.

Ashi hayaki	Aki kaze ya	Tōyama ni
Chōchin wo ou	Ganchū no mono	Hi no ataritaru
Samusa kana	Mina haiku	Kare-no kana
Kyoshi	*Kyoshi*	*Kyoshi*
(1874–)		

ARTESIAN WELL

Bathed with lunar light,
Jewels from artesian well
Scatter silvery bright.

CHERRY–FLOWERS

Cherry-flowers are now
In full bloom, yet no petal
Flutters from the bough.

SUMMER MOON

By the wind-bell, there
Hangs the moon against the deep
Blue so round and fair.

Tsuki abite	Saki michite	Fūrin ni
Tama kuzure-oru	Koboreru hana no	Ōki na tsuki no
Fukei kana	Nakari keri	Kakari keri
Kyoshi	*Kyoshi*	*Kyoshi*

SUMMER NIGHT

In the summer night
Someone at my lodging house
Comes to put out the light.

ON THE DEATH OF SHIKI

Shiki passed away
At the budding moonlit hour
Of the seventeenth day.

SPRING NIGHT

By the lantern-light
The wind is seen that scatters
Cherries fair and white.

Mijikayo ya
Hi wo keshi ni kuru
Yado no mono
   Kyoshi
      (1874–   )

Shiki yuku ya
Jūshichinichi no
Tsuki ake ni
   Kyoshi

Chōchin ni
Rakka no hana no
Miyuru kana
   Kyoshi

VIOLET

Violet is fair
Beside the little shadow
Of the earth-crust there !

THE CRISP SPRING AIR

Trunks of pine-tree stand
In the crisp spring air as they
Grow out of the sand.

THE FALLEN LEAVES

Unlike is each sound
I hear of dry leaves as I
Tread them on the ground.

Tsuchi kure no
Chisaki hikage no
Sumire kana
  Kyoshi

Harusamu ya
Suna yori ideshi
Matsu no miki
  Kyoshi

Fumiariku
Ochiba no oto no
Chigaikeri
  Kyoshi

85

TEA-PLANTS

By the lantern, white
Are the blossoms of tea-plants
Near the road at night.

VIOLENT GALE

In the upper sky
Where towers the cloud, the violent
Gale is passing by.

MIGRATING BIRDS

Cloudlets move on high
With their hurried feet, and birds
Go across the sky.

Chōchin ni
Cha no hana shiroki
Yomichi kana
   Hekigodō
     (1873-1937)

Uazora ni
Hayate fukuran
Kumo no mine
   Hekigodō

Kumo hayaki
Sora ni narikeri
Tori wataru
   Hekigodō

MOONLIT SHOWER

Underneath the bright
Moonlit shower I hear its soft
Whisper in the night.

IN AUTUMN

Oh, this road, we pass,
Will lead us to Mount Fuji
Through the pampas-grass.

MAPLE LEAVES

The garden is now
Left unswept for maple leaves
Flutter from their bough.

Tsuki no ame	Kono michi no	Momiji chiru
Shizuka ni ame wo	Fuji ni nariyuku	Konogoro niwa wo
Kiku yo kana	Suzuki kana	Hakazu ari
Hekigodō	*Hekigodō*	*Hekigodō*

WINTER MOON

Chilly is the bright
Moon that paints the shadowy trees
On the snow so white.

THE KARASAKI'S PINE

Ah, alas, here soon
Karasaki's pine will die,
But how bright the moon !

AUTUMN INSECTS

Little village here
Is sleeping, lulled by insects
Singing sweet and clear.

Kangetsu ya	Karasaki no	Mushi no naka ni
Kikage wo egaku	Matsu wa karuruni	Nete shimaitaru
Yuki no ue	Tsukiyo kana	Komura kana
Kubutsu	*Kubutsu*	*Getto* (1879–)
(1875–)		

88

WINTER TEMPEST

Winter tempest blew :
The mountains and the rivers
Lost each lovely hue.

SUMMER HEAT

Oh, how small, my sweet,
Is your painted parasol
In the intense heat !

NEW YEAR'S DAY

O, how calm and so
Quiet is this New Year's Day —
Dawn with fallen snow !

Nowaki shite
Iro ushinaeru
San ka kana
   Getto

Retsujitsu ni
Kimi ga higasa no
Chiisasa yo
   Seihō (1882–   )

Ganjitsu no
Yuki ni aketaru
Shizuka kana
   Seihō

MOUNT FUJI

Oh, Suruga plain !
There great Mount Fuji rises
High above the grain.

WISTERIAS

In the twilight gloom
Of the redwood and the pine
Fair wisterias bloom.

CLEAR SPRING

As I sip the clear
Water of the spring and the waves
Come rippling near.

Suruga no ya
Ōkina Fuji ga
Mugi no ue
   Arō (1879–   )

Matsu sugi no
Kuraki ga naka ya
Fuji no hana
   Shihōta

Kuchi yareba
Nami tatami kuru
Shimizu kana
   Haku-un
      (1877–   )

CUCKOO

Oh, the cuckoo's tune
Is sweet and here the woman's
Bath is still at noon.

LONG AGO

Ah, 'twas long ago
First I fought upon this mount ; —
Now the grasses grow !

HEAVY SNOW

Oh, how quietly
And how still the heavy snow
Fades into the sea !

Uguisu ya	Imawa mukashi	Ōyuki no
Hiru shizukanaru	Hatsujin no yamaya	Umi ni kiekomu
On-na buro	Kusashigeru	Shizukasa yo
Rinpū	*Chūon*	*Sazamami*
(1870–)	(1879–)	(1870–)

MAPLE LEAVES

Falling maples, their
Colors float continuously
Gay and bright and fair.

THE BALMY SPRING DAY

Soothed by the serene
Balminess of spring I fell
Asleep on the green.

AT SUNSET

Master of the house
Enjoys the west-sun over
Pomegranates on boughs.

Chiru momiji	Nodokasa ni	An nushi no
Iro tsuranari-te	Nete shimai keri	Nishihi tanoshimu
Nagare keri	Kusa no ue	Zakuro kana
Bujin (1877–)	*Tōyōjō*	*Tōyōjō*
	(1878–)	

INSECT SYMPHONY

Over the symphony
Of the insects, blows the breeze
Intermittently.

SPRING HILLS

Spring hills disappear
Sinking behind the pine-grove
As I go anear.

THE RIVER OF HEAVEN

Fed by many a bright
Brooklet, runs the River of Heaven
Deep into the night.

Mushi no koe	Yuku ni tsure	Ama no kawa
Ori ori wataru	Matsu ni shizuminu	Edagawa dekite
Arashi kana	Haru no yama	Fukeni-keri
Seiran	*Seiran*	*Hanamino*
(1876–)		(1881–)

FROM THE HILL TOP

Some one from below
Too is looking at the storm
Of the cherry snow.

MAPLE–SPRAY

The view, far away,
Is obstructed by the bright
Maple's single spray !

LOCUSTS

Being harrowed by
Rice-cutting, into the water
Locusts blindly fly.

Shitakara mo	Enbō wo	Kari sebame
Miagete iru ya	Saegiru momiji	Rarete inago no
Hanafubuki	Isshi kana	Mizu e tobi
Hakugetsu	*Hakugetsu*	*Tenshin*
(1882–)		

SPRING WATER

I rinse out the fine
Silken garments, making spring
Water gleam and shine.

GREEN BREEZE

There green breeze dies out
Making a little hollow
Over the rice-sprout.

FIRECRACKER

Color of the sky
Has thrice changed by firecracker
Shooting up on high.

Shunsui wo	Ao arashi	Sora no iro
Kagayakashitsutsu	Sanae kubomete	Sando kawarishi
Yusugi keri	Kie ni keri	Hanabi kana
Kisu	*Bansui*	*Chishi*

PAMPAS-GRASS

Through the pampas-grass
That sways and dances gently
In the breeze, I pass.

SUNSET

Oh, how piercing red
Is the autumn setting sun,
On the coxcomb's head !

THE SNOW-BALL

There comes the snow-ball
One after another
Over the high wall.

Fukare iru
Suzuki no naka wo
Tōri keri
Seireishi

Keitō ni
Shimitsuku akino
Irihi kana
Gochu

Yuki tsubute
Shikiri ni hei wo
Koetekuru
Toshio

96

BEACH UMBRELLAS

Beach umbrellas stand
In view among the piling
Rocks along the strand.

GENTIAN

Gentian's flowers are found
Here and there, stepped upon,
In the hunting ground.

TELLINA-SHELL

As I stretch my hand
To gather sweet tellina,
Waves come to the strand.

Kasanareru	Rindō no	Hirowan to
Iwa no hazama no	Hana fumare ari	Sureba nami kuru
Higasa kana	Kari no niwa	Sakuragai
Kyodo	*Seishi*	*Kayo*

COXCOMB–BLOOM

Underneath the blue
Autumn sky, the coxcomb-bloom
Flings its violent hue.

INQUIRY

"Chestnut gatherers ?" they
Inquired of us with smiles
When we asked the way.

ON WAY TO MANCHURIA

In the rain at fall
From the shabby coach I view
The New Capital.

Akibare ya	Michi toeba	Akiame ya
Hageshiki iro no	Kurihiroi ka to	Borobasha de miru
Hageitō	Toware-keri	Sin kokuto
Kenkenshi	*Suichikukyo*	*Suichikukyo*

IN AUTUMN

Mounting o'er the broad
Stone among the fallen leaves,
Runs the little road.

FLY

Smoothly carried by
A stream of electric fan
Floats a little fly.

MEIJI ERA

Snows are falling on
The earth : into the distance
Meiji has gone.

Banseki e	Hae hitotsu	Furuyuki ya
Michi no noritaru	Tobi nagarekeri	Meiji wa toku
Ochiba kana	Senpuki	Narini-keri
Tōkōshi	*Kishi*	*Kusadao*
(1889–)		

NIGHTINGALES

Deep between the dales
Wrapped with veils of evening mist,
Sing the nightingales.

MOONLIT NIGHT

In the moonlit sky
There the mounts of inky clouds
Stand abreast on high.

IN THE GROVE OF PLUM-
FLOWERS

Night begins to come,
And the darkness falls at once
In the grove of plum.

Tani fukaku	Makkuro no	Kuresomete
Uguisu nakeri	Kumo no minetatsu	Niwaka ni kurenu
Yūgasumi	Tsukiyo kana	Umebayashi
Shuoshi	*Nansō*	*Sōjō* (1905–)
(1892–)	(1884–)	

IRISES

There the waters flow
With the blooming irises
Reflected below.

SPRING NIGHT

The night is falling
For children, and in a distance
The frogs are calling.

SNOWY MORN

In the morn I go
Striding over the bamboo
Broken by the snow.

Hana shobu
Utsureru mizu no
Nagarekeri
Takeshi
(1889–)

Kodomora ni
Yoru ga kitareri
Tō gaeru
Seison
(1892–)

Yukiore no
Take wo mataide
Tōri-keri
Shasui

A BUTTERFLY

Though for study, I
Close my eyes to put the pin
Through a butterfly.

WEEPING WILLOW

Willow threads are lined
Up so neatly as they sway
In the gentle wind.

THE ACORNS

Making a clear sound
For gathering children, acorns
Drop down to the ground.

Gakumon no	Fukaretsutsu	Hirou ko ni
Chō ni harisasu	Yanagi no ito no	Otoshite ochiru
Me wo tsumuri	Soroikeri	Kono mi kana
Shizuko	*Kimiko*	*Shokyoku*

BON DANCE

Dancing rings become
Larger and larger with quick
Beats of the snare-drum.

AUTUMN EVENING

Autumn evening
I came into a straight road
In my traveling.

NIGHTINGALE

There the nightingale
Is heard within the whirling
Sound of violent gale.

Odoru wa no	Mattsugu na	Okaze no
Futoritsutsu-ari	Michi ni idekeri	Naka no uguisu
Shime daiko	Aki no kure	Kikoe ori
Toyoshi	*Soju*	*Fusei* (1885–)
(1882–)		

NEW YEAR'S WINE

Pour the New Year's wine
Till the gold chrysanthemum-crest
Floats with clear outline.

FALLING CHERRY-FLOWERS

Falling petals of fair
Cherries seem to stay a while
In the blue mid air.

FALLING LEAVES

With a rustling sound
Falling leaves pursue and pass
Others on the ground.

Toso tsuge yo
Kiku no gomon no
Ukabu made
   Aoi (1873–1941)

Nakazora ni
Tomaran to suru
Rakka kana
   Teijo

Karakara to
Ochiba oikite
Oikoshinu
   Tatsuko

PART TWO

EXPERIMENTS IN ENGLISH

BY SHŌSON

A PEPPER-POD

EXPERIMENTS IN ENGLISH

CAMELLIA-FLOWER

Brushing the leaves, fell
A camellia into the soft
Darkness of the well.

THE BLUE POOL

Luminous and cool
Is the way the pebble sinks
Into the blue pool.

CRIMSON DRAGONFLY

Crimson dragonfly,
Glancing the water, casts rings
As it passes by.

CALLA-LILY

Cast by morning light
A stamen's shadow is black
On the calla white.

IN DAFFODIL-FIELD

Flowered is her hem
Ankle-deep in daffodils
As she gathers them.

PLOWING

Purple cinquefoil
Turns before the plow with fresh
Fragrance of the soil.

AT PARTING

Oh, at parting now,
Let me speak by breaking
A lilac from the bough.

BREEZE AND ANEMONES

On the grass the breeze,
Resting, leans upon the blades
Against anemones.

SUMMER TREES

Shade of summer trees
Almost reaches to my desk
With the gentle breeze.

THE RAINBOW

From the clearing space
Arched with rainbow, falls the rain
On a lifted face.

GENTLE WIND

Over the soft green
Of the wheat, into the pine,
Gentle wind is seen.

AT YOSEMITE FALL

Silver is the call
Of the dipper thrown aslant
On the waterfall.

THE POPPY-FIELD

Circling again
Flies the hill-side poppy-field
Far, far from the train.

IRISES

Irises on their stalks
Gently bend before the breeze,
Bordering the walks.

AT TACOMA, WASHINGTON

Shadows from the hills
Lengthen half-across a field
Of gold daffodils.

THE RAIN

Tenderly again
On the peony I hear
Whispers of the rain.

AT SUNSET

Peaceful is the sea
That with sunset flush and gold
Leaves the eve to me.

THE BUTTERFLY

Blow along the grass
Gently, wind, the butterflies
Flutter in a mass.

CRIMSON DRAGONFLY

Crimson dragonfly,
As it lights, sways together
With the leaf of rye.

THE PURPLE GRAPE

I forego the best
Clusters of the purple grape
To the hornet's nest.

THE LIZARD

A lizard swam over
The undulating waves
Of the fresh green clover.

A BUTTERFLY

Over the hedge-trees
A butterfly is carried
Away by the breeze.

KATYDID

In moon-light, half-hid
With the silhouettes of leaves,
Twits the katydid.

THE POPPY-FIELD

Coming into the wide
Highway, still the sun is high
On the poppy side.

IRISES

Irises in bloom,
Soon the white one too will fade
Into the gathering gloom.

AN INSECT

Keeping in sweet chime,
An insect rings a golden bell
Two and three a-time.

NIGHTINGALE

Lovely is your throat,
Nightingale, who scorns the cage
With a golden note.

SWEET PEAS

Tenderly sweet peas
Hold each other with their green
Tendrils in the breeze.

LAST NIGHT MOON

In the summer sky
Hangs the last night moon, so faint
Yet so clear on high.

THE SPRING WATER

I drink — listening
To the sound of the water
Rising from the spring.

LOTUS FLOWER

Pink among the white,
With a "pong" the lotus blooms
In the blue dawn-light.

SPRING BREEZE

Green is the spring breeze
Tangled among the bending
Branches of the trees.

MAPLE LEAVES

Bright and beautiful
Are the maples reflected
All over the pool.

THE BUTTERFLY

Each time breezes pass,
The butterfly shifts its place
On the flower in grass.

THE RAIN

Hurriedly runs rain
Toward the sunlit grain-field
Half-across the plain.

AT DENSON, ARKANSAS

'Gainst the inky sky
The lightning paints the great oak
As it flashes by.

THE MISSISSIPPI RIVER

Under the low grey
Winter skies water pushes
Water on its way.

THE BRIGHT MOON

On its back the white
Cloudlet carries the bright moon
In the autumn night.

HYDRANGEA

Underneath the eaves
Large hydrangea's clustered disks
Overbrim the leaves.

FROM THE MOUNTAIN-TOP

Through the sea of cloud
The roar of the cataract
Resounds clear and loud.

HARVEST MOON

Broken, broken, yet
Perfect is the harvest moon
On the rivulet.

INSECT'S SONG

The sound of the shower
Blankets the autumn insects
Singing in their bower.

WHITE SWANS

White swans, one or two,
Draw near, pushing the water
For the food I threw.

AT YOSEMITE PARK

Cataract's white sheet
Cleaves the lush foliage
Many a hundred feet !

A FALLING ACORN

With a chilly, light
Sound a falling acorn rolls
Down the roof at night.

AUTUMN SKY

The autumn day drew
To a close with skies — keen,
Clear, and cobalt blue.

SUMMER RAIN

Oh, the summer rain
Sprinkles lightly on the star-
Spangled pool again.

SUDDEN SHOWER

Wet with sudden shower,
Flutteringly a butterfly
Comes into my bower.

DAISIES

Day turns into night,
Yet skies remain blue, above
Daisies dancing white.

SUMMER SHOWER

The green breeze passes,
Accompanied by summer shower
Across the grasses.

POPPIES

Poppies on the hill
Pave a meadow as they spread
Down along the rill.

BUMBLEBEE

A large bumblebee
Tumbles down, clasping the flower
Of the lemon-tree.

THE PERSIMMONS

How delicious now,
These persimmons left alone
On the broken bough.

FIREFLIES

Glimmering appear
Grass-leaves in the firefly-cage
Slender and linear.

SPRING BREEZE

As it passes by
The breeze wakes the green wavelets
Over the young rye.

IN THE GARDEN

With the mattock I
Dig the garden where the cloud's
Shadow passes by.

SUNSET AND POPPIES

With the sunset gold
A field of poppy merges
In a continuous fold.

A DIRGE FOR A SOLDIER

Moving in one big sway
Flower of winter peony
Scatter bright and gay.

FISH–RIPPLES

On the placid stream
By withering reeds, fish-ripples
Spread out with a gleam.

PALOWANIA–LEAF

Glistening in the sun,
Falls a *kiri*-leaf following
Its shadow alone.

IN THE GARDEN

On the bench I wait
For the second gust to come
Through the garden gate.

AT NIGHT

Suddenly I met
With a fragrance in the dark,
Silver mignonette.